GREAT TENORS OF THE TWENTIETH CENTURY

FROM

CARUSO

TO

PAVAROTTI

BY

ANNE KRIKLER

Grosvenor House
Publishing Limited

This book is published by
Grosvenor House Publishing Ltd
28-30 High Street, Guildford, Surrey, GU1 3HY.
www.grosvenorhousepublishing.co.uk

A CIP record for this book
is available from the British Library

ISBN 978-1-907211-84-3

DEDICATION

This book is dedicated to the memory of my mother

I would also like to express my gratitude to my dear husband Dennis, who gave me immense support with great patience and kindness

ACKNOWLEDGEMENT

I thank Mussadaque Butt from Cube Technology for his very helpful technical assistance.

PICTURE REFERENCES

The pictures added in this book are referenced from the websites mentioned below:

www.lastfm.com
www.google.co.uk
www.wikipedia.org

GREAT TENORS OF THE TWENTIETH CENTURY

TABLE OF CONTENTS

TABLE OF CONTENTS

PERSONALIA

I was born in Gleiwitz, Germany in 1935. In 1936 my family immigrated to South Africa because of the advent of the Nazi regime. We settled in Cape Town where I grew up and was educated. In Cape Town there was good opera enhanced by internationally renowned tenors and my mother, a lover of opera, took me to these performances, thereby instilling in me the same passion. In 1955 I married my husband who was a doctor at Groote Schuur Hospital. While he had specialist training in London we frequented Covent Garden and on a European trip were able to visit La Scala, La Fenice in Venice and the Vienna State Opera. We then emigrated to Salisbury, Southern Rhodesia where among other things I became a member of the National Arts Council and was responsible for Music. In 1966 my husband was appointed a consultant cardiologist in London and we settled here with our children. Since living here we have had the opportunity to take advantage of the great music, especially opera, available here as well as on the continent, New York and Sydney.

Also by Anne Krikler: The Magic of Music in Film (2007)

PREFACE

Opera has been around for several hundred years but has assumed its contemporary format since the days of Mozart. It was during the nineteenth century that the separate expression of the tenor voice became significant and the most famous component derived from the Polish-born Jean de Reszke.

Opera became more available to the wider audience in the twentieth century through development of recordings, having previously been restricted only to the small numbers of the elite who lived in towns and especially big cities with opera houses. The opera house remains the essential focus of operatic performance, but especially with the progressive improvement of recording techniques the great voices of today can be heard in the home as well as more recently in open air venues.

The purpose of this book is to analyse the voices of tenors from Caruso onwards. There are numerous talented tenors culminating in the late great Luciano Pavarotti. While these are discussed, this book is not intended to deal with tenors who have exclusive interest in specialist tones, which is why Lauritz Melchior and his like, the "Heldentenors", who concentrate on Wagnerian opera, are not discussed. What is most encouraging is the arrival of several younger tenors whose qualities show great promise and indicate that the role of the tenor provides pleasure today.

THE EARLY DEVELOPMENT
OF TENORS

In the early eighteenth century, after his experience in Italy, where George Frederick Handel was able to distinguish tenors from castrati, in his London years he was able to compose songs for tenors, mostly Italians. Subsequently he concentrated on using British tenors. The next major step was taken by Wolfgang Amadeus Mozart in Salzburg and Vienna, whom we now recognise as the first, indeed most successful, and still admired, composer of opera who remains respected and indeed beloved to this day.

An important singer was the tenor Gilbert-Louis Duprez who achieved a high C in Rossini's opera William Tell, in performances in the early nineteenth century. The Paris Opera was so impressed that it gave him a contract to perform in operas by the leading composers of the time. He was emulated by Enrico Tamberlik, noted for his attempt, not always successful, also to achieve a high C, though not always able to obtain a large fee.

Other important composers of opera, a little later, were Hector Berlioz and Giacomo Meyerbeer. A major tenor much used by Meyerbeer was Giovanni Matteo de Camdia who adopted the stage name of Mario, who performed throughout Europe and was probably the first European tenor to perform in New York. Jean-Alexandre Talazac was a successful French tenor who had favoured French composers but who had an unfortunately brief career as he died at the age of 45. Angelo Masini, famed for his ability to reach high notes, was an important figure who performed in much of Europe and also in South America. The Spanish tenor Manuel Garcia was the first of his family to have a major career and was comparable to the best of the Italian voices of the day like Masini; who was also rivalled by Julian Dayarre - he favoured Giuseppe Verdi's operas.

These were all nineteenth century tenors, some active during the career of Jean de Reszke, who was born in Warsaw in 1859, to an important Polish family, some of whom were also talented singers, notably his brother Edouard as well as his sister Josephine. Jean made his debut at La Fenice in Venice in 1874. Two years later he made his Parisian debut in The Force of Destiny. Until then some had considered him to be a baritone but it then became clear that he was a tenor. It was at this stage that he settled in France and made Paris his base.

De Reszke made his American debut at the Metropolitan Opera House in 1891 and for the next ten years sang with tremendous success in the United States. He proved extremely popular everywhere and in addition to the admiration for his singing was loved by all for his attractive personality. Unfortunately he was much troubled by frequent respiratory illnesses which forced him to give up singing at the height of his success when 55 years old. Thereafter he became a teacher; he had made a very good recording of The Pearlfishers by Georges Bizet with his brother Edouard; only one other recording was made in 1901, but the technical quality was poor.

He had an immense repertoire covering all the important roles which he could sing in Polish, Russian, French and Italian. In addition he spoke English and German well, which enhanced his ability as a teacher. De Reszke died in 1925; a little known anecdote was the use of his surname on a brand of cigarettes.

A contemporary of de Reszke was the Italian tenor Fernando de Lucia who was born in 1860; he also died in 1925. He made his debut at the San Carlo theatre in Naples in 1885, and made many appearances in Europe, South America and the United States. Giacomo Puccini chose de Lucia to star as Rodolfo in La Boheme. He sang at Caruso's funeral in Naples in 1921; unlike de Reszke he made a large number of recordings but remains less well known than him.

THE MAJOR
OPERA HOUSES

THE ROYAL OPERA HOUSE, COVENT GARDEN

The Royal Opera House derives from the Theatre Royal, Covent Garden, from a licence granted in 1660 by Charles II, giving Covent Garden and The Theatre Royal Drury Lane the right to operate as theatres. The first theatre was only built in 1728. It was preceded by a company in Lincolns Inn Fields. George Frederick Handel became musical director in 1719; his first season of opera at Covent Garden was in 1734.

The theatre was destroyed by fire in 1808 and rebuilt the following year. In 1847 the auditorium was completely remodelled and reopened as the Royal Italian Opera the same year with a performance of Rossini's Semiramide.

In 1856 the theatre was again destroyed by fire and a completely new building, which still remains as part of the present theatre reopened in1858 with a performance of Meyerbeer's Les Huguenots. That year the opera company moved from the Theatre Royal, Drury Lane, to Covent Garden. The theatre became the Royal Opera House in 1892. The house closed as a performing place during the First World War and became a furniture depository. In 1934-6 Thomas Beecham was music director. During the Second World War it became a dance hall. The Royal Opera House reopened in February 1946, and in January 1947 the company gave as its first performance Bizet's Carmen. In 1996 a major reconstruction was started and completed in 2000.

ENGLISH NATIONAL OPERA

In 1896 a series of opera recitals were held at the Old Vic theatre where a company was established in 1912. In 1931 Sadlers Wells theatre opened with the Vic-Wells Opera Company. During the Second World War Sadlers Wells was closed and the company toured the country. Sadlers Wells reopened in 1945 with Peter Grimes by Benjamin Britten, the first English opera composer since Purcell and in 1968 moved to the Coliseum; in 1974 it became the English National Opera (ENO), which presents operas only in English.

LA SCALA

The Teatro alla Scala in Milan, by night

La Scala was inaugurated in Milan in 1778. Two years previously a plan for this new theatre had been accepted by Empress Maria Theresa. The structure was renovated in 1907 but in 1943. La Scala was severely damaged by bombing. In May 1946 it reopened with a memorable concert conducted by Arturo Toscanini with the soprano Renata Tebaldi which created a sensation.

La Scala hosted the first production of many famous operas. It had a variable relationship with Giuseppe Verdi who objected to some of the productions of his operas but who later had his Requiem as well as Otello and Falstaff premiered there.

Between 2002 and 2004 it underwent major renovation and reopened on 7 December 2004 with a production of Salieri's Europa riconasciuta which originally had been performed at the inauguration of La Scala in 1778. Among its principal conductors were Arturo Toscanini, Varlo Maria Giulani. Claudio Abbado, Riccardo Muti and Daniel Barenboim. Its premieres included Norma, by Bellini, Maria Stuarda by Gaetano Donizetti, Nabucco by Verdi and Madama Butterfly by Puccini.

LA FENICE

The interior of La Fenice in 1837

This is the cutest opera house I have visited, located in the most beautiful city in Italy. The construction began in June 1790 and was completed in May 1792 and the first production was I Giuochi di Agrigento by Giovanni Paisiello. Rossini and Bellini had two operas produced at La Fenice and after an absence of 17 years, Donizetti returned to Venice in 1836.

In December 1836 the theatre was destroyed by fire but was quickly rebuilt and reopened in December 1837. Verdi had a performance of Ernani in1844 and over the next thirteen years La Fenice held the premieres of Attila, Rigoletto and La Traviata.

On 29 January 1996 it was again burned down but it was rebuilt and reopened on 14 December 2003 and its first opera production was La Traviata in November 2004.

TEATRO DI SAN CARLO

Teatro San Carlo, interior prior to 1916

This famous opera house in Naples was inaugurated on 4 November 1737 but destroyed by fire on 12 February 1816 but was quickly rebuilt, and on 12 January 1817 reopened with Johann Simon Mayr's Il sogno di Partenope. Stendahl wrote "There is nothing in all Europe....comparable to this theatre.....it enraptures the soul."

In 1943 San Carlo suffered from bombing. The theatre was quickly repaired by the Allied occupation forces and reopened within six months on 16 December that year.

In the nineteenth century Neapolitan opera enjoyed great success all over Europe, and Naples became the capital of European music. International composers who favoured Naples included Haydn, Johann Christian Bach and Gluck. From 1815 to 1822 Rossini was artistic director; he was followed by Donizetti. Regular singers included the Spaniard Manuel Garcia and Gilbert Duprez. Giuseppe Verdi composed operas for San Carlo, including Luisa Miller and Alvira. By the end of the nineteenth century and into the twentieth Giacomo Puccini, Pietro Mascagni, Leoncavallo and Giordano had their operas produced there also. While San Carlo has continued to function it has been overtaken in importance by other houses.

VERONA ARENA

Verona Arena in 2009

Inside the Verona Arena

The Verona Arena is a Roman amphitheatre which was built in AD 30 for shows and games. The round façade was originally composed of limestone but after an earthquake in 1117 the stone was reused elsewhere. Some operatic performances were mounted during the 1850s, but these continued on a low level. The first major opera was Verdi's Aida which was performed on 10 August 1913, to commemorate the centenary of his birth; Puccini and Mascagni were present. Since then summer seasons of opera have been mounted annually except during the first and second world wars. Since the Second World War singers have included Giuseppi di Stefano, Maria Callas, Tito Gobbi and Renata Tebaldi.

VIENNA STATE OPERA

In the mid-nineteenth century it was decided to establish the Vienna State Opera (Wiener Staatsoper). Work on its building was started in 1862 and completed eight years later. The foundation stone was laid on 20 May 1863. The opening performance was of Mozart's Don Giovanni. An early and key figure was the conductor Gustav Mahler (an important composer) who radically improved the scenery and cultivated a new generation of singers, such as Anna Bahr-Mildenburg and Selma Kurz.

On 12 March 1945 the building was burned down by an American bombardment; the opera was temporarily housed at the Theatre an der Wien and the Vienna Volksoper. On 5 November 1955 the State Opera reopened with Fidelio by Beethoven which was conducted by Karl Bohm. An important figure in the reconstruction was the Austrian-Jewish conductor Josef Krips who had miraculously survived the Nazi era. Until his death in 1974 Krips was one of the most important conductors and music directors of the State Opera.

Herbert von Karajan, an eminent post-war conductor, introduced the practice of performing operas in their original language and began collaboration with La Scala in Milan. The State Opera produces up to 60 operas a year, giving about 200 performances. The current musical director is Seiji Ozawa.

BAYREUTH FESTSPIELHAUS

Bayreuth Festspielhaus, as seen today

This opera house is dedicated mainly to the performance of operas by Richard Wagner and is the venue for the annual Bayreuth festival. The design was adapted by Wagner from an unrealized project by Gottfried Semper who had designed the Dresden opera house, The foundation stone was laid on Wagner's birthday, 22 May 1872, and the building was opened with a complete four-opera cycle of the Ring of the Niebelung on 13-17 August 1876. The festspielhaus remains the venue of the annual festival. Its reputation has been marred by the close relationship of many of the Wagner family with Adolf Hitler and the Nazi philosophy.

DRESDEN SEMPER OPERA HOUSE

In the first place the opera chorus was founded by Carl Maria von Weber. The House was first built in 1841 by Gottfried Semper. It had to be rebuilt after a fire destroyed it in 1849. The architect of the new opera house was Semper's son Manfred and was completed in 1878 and is a prime example of "Dresden baroque" architecture. It is situated in the theatre square close to the bank of the River Elbe. The house held the world premiere of Richard Wagner's Rienzi, The Flying Dutchman and Tannhauser. Nine of the operas of Richard Strauss made their first stage appearances at the Semper, among them Salome, Der Rosenkavalier and Elektra. There was a jubilant reception for the opera Dead Man Walking by Heinrich Schutz.

In February 1945 the building was destroyed by allied bombing. On 13 February 1985 the Semper was rebuilt exactly as it had been before the war but with modern internal improvements. The opening production was Weber's Der Freischutz.

Conductors associated with the Semper include Carl Maria von Weber, Richard Wagner, Fritz Busch and Karl Bohm. Among the singers have been Bernd Aldenhoff, Erna Sack and Hermann Wedekind.

The Semper is one of the highlights of any visit to Dresden.

THE LEIPZIG OPERA

The Leipzig Opera, established in 1683, is the third oldest opera house in Europe. Since 1766 music has been provided by the Leipzig Gewandhaus orchestra which in its time was one of the leading orchestras in the world. The previous theatre was inaugurated on 28 January 1868. From 1886 to 1888 Gustav Mahler was the second conductor; Arthur Nikisch was his superior.

The theatre was destroyed, as were all Leipzig's theatres by an air raid on 3 December 1943. Construction of the new opera house began in 1956 and it was inaugurated on 8 October 1960 with a performance of Wagner's The Mastersingers of Nuremberg.

In May 2008 Alexander von Mararvic was appointed music director and Peter Konwitschny as principal director of productions

BERLIN STATE OPERA

Staatsoper Unter den Linden, 2003

In 1741 Frederick II commissioned the original building which was inaugurated on 7 December 1742 with a performance of Carl Heinrich Graun's Cleopatra e Cesare. On 18 August 1843 the opera house was destroyed by fire. The rebuilt House opened in 1844 with a performance of Meyerbeer's Ein Feldlager in Schlesien.

At the end of the nineteenth and the beginning of the twentieth century conductors included Felix von Weingartner, Richard Strauss and Leo Blech. In the nineteen twenties conductors included Wilhelm Furtwangler, Erich Kleiber, Otto Klemperer and Bruno Walter.

The Opera House underwent extensive renovation and reopened in April 1928 with Mozart's Magic Flute. After 1933 Jewish musicians were excluded. During the Third Reich the main conductors were Robert Heger, Herbert von Karajan and Johannes Schuler.

In 1941 the Opera House was bombed but reopened on 12 December 1942. In 1944 the Staatsoper was closed by Goebbels when he proclaimed "Total War". On 3 February 1945 the House was once again bombed, this time to destruction. It only moved back to its original home after rebuilding in 1955, having used a variety of other halls in the meantime. In 1990 the State Opera was officially renamed Staatsoper Unter den Linden and in 1992 Daniel Barenboim was appointed conductor and in 1992 was elected conductor for life.

DEUTSCHE OPER BERLIN

The house was inaugurated in 1912 and was destroyed during the war. On 24 September 1961 it was re-inaugurated and has become Berlin's largest opera house. From its beginning in Bismarckstrasse it had featured the major works of the nine-teenth and early twentieth century composers including Wagner, Verdi, Puccini and Strauss, among others. It has held 112 world premieres. Important conductors have included Bruno Walter, and its most important directors included Walter Felsenstein and Gotz Friedrich.

KROLL OPERA HOUSE

The Kroll Opera House, about 1850

The Kroll Opera House was an opera building in Berlin. The previous entertainment venue built in 1844 was redeveloped as an opera house in 1851. It was based on the Kroll Wintergarten in Breslau which had been founded in 1837. During the 1920s its resident conductor was Otto Klemperer, under whose auspices two world premieres of works by Paul Hindemith and Arnold Schoenberg were produced.

After the Reichstag fire in 1933 the Kroll became the seat of the Reichstag. The building was destroyed by Allied bombing on 22 November 1943 and its ruins were demolished in 1961. No attempt was made to revive the Kroll Opera House.

THE BERLIN OPERA

This Berlin Opera House which was built between 1911 and 1912 opened on 7 November 1912 with Beethoven's Fidelio. In 1935 the building was remodelled but that year its general manager Carl Ebert emigrated due to the Nazi regime. The opera house was destroyed on 23 November 1943; after the war Ebert returned as general manager.

The new building was completed on 24 September 1981 when the first production was Mozart's Don Giovanni. Past conductors have included Bruno Walter, Lorin Maazel and Christian Thielemann.

PARIS OPERA

The Opera National de Paris is known as the Palais Garnier after its architect, Charles Garnier. It was built between 1862 and 1875 and is a large building with a vast stage with space for up to 450 artists. It is a beautiful ornate building which is decorated with friezes, columns, and winged figures as well as other statues and embellishments. This richness continues inside with velvet, gold leaf, and nymphs and cherubs. The auditorium's central chandelier weighs over 6 tons, and the ceiling was painted by Marc Chagall in 1964.

In 1988 opera performances were transferred to the newly-built Opera Bastille, and the Palais Garnier is now devoted to ballet.

TEATRO COLON

Teatro Colón at night

In the nineteenth century Argentina became very prosperous and opera flourished in many small theatres in Buenos Aires, with numerous touring companies from Europe. The first Teatro Colon building opened on 27 April 1857 with Verdi's La Traviata, just four years after its Italian premiere. It starred Enrico Tamberlik as Alfredo and Sofia Vera Lorini as Violetta. The theatre was designed by Carlos Enrique Pelligrini, father of the future President of Argentina.

The cornerstone of a new building to replace the earlier house was laid in 1889 but it only opened on 25 May 1908 with Verdi's Aida, and it quickly became world-famous, rivalling La Scala and the Metropolitan opera. It hosted great composers like Stravinsky, Richard Strauss and Camille Saint-Saens; conductors included Arturo Toscanini, Ernest Ansermet, Thomas Beecham and Karl Bohm. There were many stars of the Italian opera like Amelita Galli-Curci, Enrico Caruso, Tito Schipa,

Beniamino Gigli, Luciano Pavarotti, Lily Pons and Fritz Wunderlich.

Before and particularly during the war years conductors Erich Kleiber, Felix Weingartner. Fritz Busch and Otto Klemperer developed the "German Season" with singers like Lauritz Melchior, Lotte Lehmann, Helen Traubel and Kirsten Flagstad.

In recent years the Teatro Colon has suffered from the political and economic disturbances in Argentina. The theatre closed in October 2006 and refurbishment is taking place with reopening due in 2010.

THE METROPOLITAN OPERA

The Metropolitan Opera House at Lincoln Center for the Performing Arts, seen from Lincoln Center Plaza

The Metropolitan Opera Association of New York City was founded in April 1880. The first Metropolitan Opera House (The Met) was located at1411 Broadway and opened on 22 October 1883 with a performance of Faust. It was gutted by fire on 22 August 1892 but was immediately rebuilt and its interior was extensively renovated in 1903. From the word go its stage facilities were seriously inadequate. The original House closed on 16 April 1966.

The Met is now located in the Lincoln Center and opened on 16 September 1966 with the world premiere of Samuel Barber's Antony and Cleopatra. The Met is noted for its excellent acoustics and all technical facilities are continuously updated.

Its present principal conductor and music director is James Levine; previous conductors include Toscanini, George Szell, Gustav Mahler and Walter Damrosch. Singers have included Luciano Pavarotti, Placido Domingo, Jean and Edouard de Reszke, Lotte Lehmann, Nellie Melba and Enrico Caruso.

The Met has now surpassed all other opera houses in importance and quality.

SAN FRANCISCO OPERA HOUSE

This is officially known as the San Francisco War Memorial Opera House in honour of those who had served during the First World War. It was built in 1932 and is also the home of the San Francisco ballet. It serves as the main opera house on the west coast of the United States. It is perhaps better known for the fact that the United Nations Charter was developed there in 1945.

Many of the famous opera singers have performed there, including those who have sung at The Met and elsewhere. A recent conductor, Peter Herman Adler, was much favoured by Luciano Pavarotti, and sometimes toured with him. The San Francisco Opera House is situated in one of the most beautiful cities in the United States.

SYDNEY OPERA HOUSE

The Opera House is situated on Bennelong Point in Sydney, New South Wales; it is located in Sydney Harbour, close to the Sydney Harbour Bridge and is surrounded on three sides by the harbour, next to the Royal Botanic Gardens.

The opera house was conceived and largely built by Jorn Utzon, the Danish architect who in 2003 received the Pritzker prize, architecture's highest honour. The opera house was made a UNESCO World Heritage Site.

The Fort Macquarie Tram Depot was demolished in 1958 and construction of the House on that site began in March 1959. The project was built in three stages: Stage 1 (1959-1963) consisted of building the upper podium; Stage 2 (1963-1967) was the construction of the outer shells; Stage 3 (1967-1973) consisted of the design and construction of the interior. Great credit is due to the consultant engineers Ove

Arup and Partners. Some of Utzon's features had to be changed before completion because the orchestra pit was cramped and dangerous to the hearing of the musicians. Towards the end of the construction, some politicians interfered with Utzon who then resigned on 28 February 1966, left partly unpaid by Davis Hughes, the new Minister for Public Works. Ove Arup actually stated that Utzon was "probably the best of any I have come across in my long experience of working with architects" and "The Opera House could become the world's foremost contemporary masterpiece if Utzon is given his head."

The Opera House was formally opened by Queen Elizabeth on 20 October 1973 and was followed by a performance of Beethoven's 9th symphony. Prior to the opening the first opera performed was Prokofiev's War and Peace on 28 September.

In 1999 there was reconciliation with Utzon who was appointed as a design consultant for future work.

Among the many international artists who have performed there were the Australian soprano Joan Sutherland and her husband Richard Bonynge the conductor.

ANNE KRIKLER

THE OPERA HOUSE THAT NEVER WAS

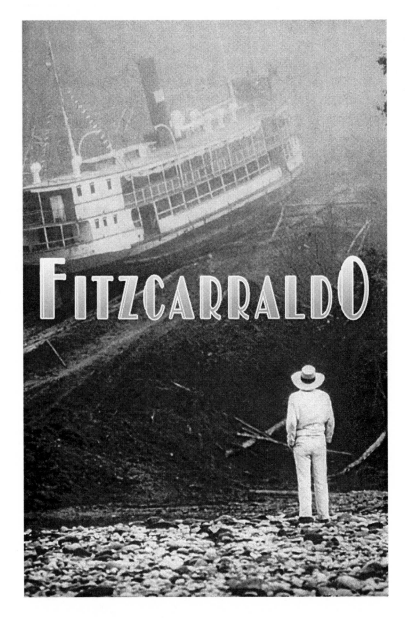

In the early part of the twentieth century Brian Sweeney Fitzgerald at the time he played his role, was an Irish rubber baron living in a small city in Peru who had a great love of opera and an indomitable spirit. Locally he was known as "Fitzcarraldo", he was a great fan of Caruso and dreamt of building an opera house in his city of Iquitos which he aimed to finance from money made from rubber. He leased an inaccessible parcel of land which was cut off from the Amazon by a treacherous set of rapids.

Fitzcarraldo bought a steamship which he sailed up the Pachitea River to reach the Ucayali, all the time he played his gramophone record of Caruso. In order to reach the land he had to have the steamship dragged from the Pachitea over a mountain to reach the Ucayali, which he hoped to achieve with the help of the local Indians. Having reached an agreement with them, they chopped down trees, constructed trolleys from logs, and then dragged the boat up the mountain. At this stage, after much chattering and singing among themselves, the Indians abruptly abandoned the work, and destroyed the trolley system so that the boat slid back to the Pachitea.

To his great dismay Fitzcarraldo realized that his dream project was thwarted. He had no option but to sail back to his starting point. As he sailed he clutched a plush red velvet chair intended for Caruso to sit on when he hoped he would come to open his opera house. Thus the opera house that never was became the subject of a remarkable film made in 1982 by the famous German movie director Werner Herzog, about a true story: Fitzcarraldo. (The film is actually derived from the real-life story of Peruvian rubber baron Carlos Fitzcarrald.)

GREAT TENORS OF THE TWENTIETH CENTURY

Enrico Caruso

BIOGRAPHY

Born Naples, 25 February, 1872; died 25 August, 1921, Naples, aged 42, most likely due to peritonitis.

Caruso's recordings in 1902 to 1920 showed how his voice developed from that of a lyric tenor into that of a classic dramatic tenor. He sang in all the great opera houses, becoming the leading tenor of the New York Metropolitan Opera. Among his most successful operas are Rigoletto in 1903 at the Metropolitan. In 1906 he performed in Carmen at the Tivoli Opera House during the San Francisco earthquake. In 1918 he married Dorothy Benjamin the daughter of a benefactor of the Metropolitan; they had a daughter Gloria a son Enrico and a second son Rodolfo. Caruso had a wide repertoire and was internationally acclaimed as the leading tenor of his day by, among others, Arturo Toscanini. He led a very glamorous and expensive lifestyle.

THE VOICE

In Caruso's singing of Vesta la Giubba from Leoncavallo's Pagliacci his tone of voice was rather monotonous, with very little variation in colour until the second part of this aria, when the colour range is ample. His singing in O Mimi, Tu Non Torni from La Boheme shows a richer and warmer tone. In Questa O Quella from Rigoletto Caruso succeeds in providing a very ample rendition; this also applies to La Donna e Mobile

In O Solo Mio, Caruso does not do justice to the feeling and excitement of this Neapolitan song, that would have been expected in his heyday. There are elements suggesting a baritone-like quality in several arias.

Caruso signing his autograph; he was obliging with fans

ROBERTO ALAGNA

BIOGRAPHY

Born 17 June 1963 in Clichy-sur-Bois, France.

Alagna is the son of Sicilian parents. Largely self-taught, he started off as a cabaret singer and also studied under Rafael Ruiz and conductor Antonio Pappano. His career took off after he won first prize in the Luciano Pavarotti international competition in Philadelphia in 1988, and followed this with his debut as Alfredo in La Traviata at Glyndebourne. He also sang this role for his debut at La Scala in 1990

After a series of performances in the lyric tenor repertoire he has moved into heavier roles like Don Jose in Carmen, Don Carlos, Cavaradossii in Tosca and Manrico. In 1994, Alagna was named musical personality of the year by the French press. In 1995 he received the Laurence Olivier award for Romeo and Juliet at Covent Garden. In 1996 he became Chevalier of the Order of Arts and Letters of his native country. He continues to sing in major opera houses in Europe and America. He is married to the great soprano Angela Gheorghiu, with whom he often performs.

THE VOICE

Alagna has a strong, basically dark, and large voice. It is steady, and he changes his ranges with ease. On the other hand, while his voice is good, it could be a little smoother and have more warmth and colour. His high range reaches its peak but is at times a little ragged. In La Boheme, for example, the voice is responsive, thereby giving us a pure and warm rendition. Alagna is clearly a talented tenor.

CARLO BERGONZI

BIOGRAPHY

Born 13 July 1924 in Vidalengo, near Parma, Italy.

Bergonzi began his vocal studies at the age of 14 but these were interrupted by wartime internment in a German camp. After the war he studied at the Boito Conservatory in Parma. Initially a baritone, after training he made his debut as a tenor in Andrea Chenier in Bari. Two years later he made his debuts at La Scala and in London, the latter as Alvaro in The Force of Destiny. His American debut at the Lyric Opera of Chicago took place in 1955; the following year he made his debut at the Metropolitan Opera as Radames in Aida. In 1957 his Covent Garden debut was again as Alvaro.

While he continued to sing throughout the 1970s his vocal qualities gradually deteriorated and he therefore concentrated on recitals. Now retired, he does some teaching.

THE VOICE

Early on in Bergonzi's singing an aria by Verdi, he started off by displaying a wobble. His voice is dark and steady in the lower register but unimpressive in the higher notes later, in a different aria his rendition had improved slightly, but there was more baritone than tenor. Nevertheless he had a large voice which he used well. His voice was surpassed by many of his contemporaries.

JUSSI BJOERLING

BIOGRAPHY

Born 5 February 1911, Borlange (Sweden); died 9 September 1960, Siaro (Sweden).

Bjoerling trained at the Royal Music Academy in Stockholm and made his professional debut at the Royal Swedish Opera in Stockholm in 1930 as the lamplighter in Manon Lescaut. In 1938 he made his first appearance at the Metropolitan Opera as Rodolfo in La Boheme. As one of the principal singers his roles included Don Ottavio in Mozart's Don Giovanni, Arnaldo in William Tell and Almaviva in Barber of Seville. Later at the Metropolitan Opera his repertoire included Manrico in Il Trovatore, Rigoletto and Aida. In December 1940 he sang the tenor part in Beethoven's Missa Solemnis in New York for Toscanini. He also made a complete recording of La Boheme with Victoria de los Angeles and Robert Merrill under the baton of Sir Thomas Beecham. Although much admired for his musicality he had limited acting ability. Unfortunately his life, and to some extent his career, was blighted by severe alcoholism. He died of heart failure at the age of 49, possibly related to alcohol-induced cardiomyopathy, a disorder that progressively damages the heart muscle.

THE VOICE

One remembers this very fine tenor with great joy: in fact, when I first heard him, I thought he was the best. He had a very velvety rich sound over his complete range; sadly this declined over the years; as happens to all singers, some sooner, others later, especially as each voice is different. Nevertheless we still have his recordings, which is important as it reminds us of his beautiful voice.

ANDREA BOCELLI

BIOGRAPHY

Born 22 September 1958, in Lajatito (Italy).

Bocelli was fascinated by the passion and storytelling of opera and dreamt of following in the footsteps of his idols Mario de Monaco, Beniamino Gigli and especially Franco Corelli. His family wanted him to study law but he retained his passion for music and he soon studied under several maestros, notably Corelli. He sang at many of the famous opera houses in a variety of roles. In 1992 he recorded a duet with Pavarotti. In 1996-7 Bocelli achieved great success with a collection of popular songs. He then switched back to opera and recorded Carmen, Cavallaria Rusticana and Pagliacci as well as several non-operatic pieces. He has received widespread personal acclaim for the whole range of his achievements which have been recognised despite his blindness.

THE VOICE

Bocelli gives a very fine rendition of Nessun Dorma in Turandot by Puccini with an especially fine high C. Basically his tone was rather darker in most of the aria. He does not sound like a spinto lyrical tenor; this characterises much of his singing of other arias as well as Neapolitan songs like O Solo Mio. (Spinto is the Italian for "pushed" and denotes a voice that is half-way between a lyric and a dramatic one). Overall he is an impressive tenor.

JOSE CARRERAS

BIOGRAPHY

Born 5 December 1946, Barcelona.

As a youngster Carreras was inspired by the voice of Mario Lanza. At the age of eight he made his first public performance singing La Donna E Mobile on Spanish National Radio; at eleven he sang in De Fallad in the boy soprano role in El Retabelo de Maese Pedro. In London he sang Maria Stuarda as well as another fifteen operas. In 1974 he sang in Rigoletto at the Vienna State Opera as well as Alfredo in La Traviata at Covent Garden and Tosca at the Metropolitan Opera. In 1987 he developed acute leukaemia but was fortunately cured. After recovery he was able to resume his career. Since 1990 he has appeared with Pavarotti and Domingo as one of the famed Three Tenors.

THE VOICE

Carreras sings Puccini's Che Gelido Mannina from La Boheme with much passion and pathos which has a silky flow as it reaches the upper register when it becomes dramatically strong and very steady; he excels in the high C. He is a very fine singer and his voice complemented those of the other two Three Tenors, receiving great acclaim.

FRANCO CORELLI

BIOGRAPHY

Born 8 April 1921 in Ancona (Italy); died 29 October 2003 in Milan.

Corelli was trained by Rita Pavoni at the Pesaro Conservatory of Music initially, and subsequently by the world-renowned Arturo Melochi. After various roles at smaller theatres he reached La Scala in 1954, as Licinio in Spontini's La Vestale opposite Maria Callas. His first appearance at Covent Garden was as Cavaradossi in Tosca in 1957. On 27 January 1961 he first appeared at the Metropolitan Opera as Manrico in Il Trovatore opposite Leontyne Price. Corelli retired in 1976 aged 55. By this time his voice was showing signs of wear and tear. He suffered a stroke in Milan where he then died.

THE VOICE

Corelli had a very good voice when singing in Donna e Mobile from Rigoletto by Verdi. He proved himself as a fine tenor and his different ranges, in particular the high C; the lower ranges were less well sung, which is a great shame.

JOSE CURA

BIOGRAPHY

Born 5 December 1962, in Rosario, Argentina.

Cura's first role was in Signorina Julia by Bibalo, which he sang in Trieste. He became famous for his canal-side performances in front of the Hotel Pulitzer in Amsterdam where he enthralled large open air audiences in a selection of famous arias; he appealed to the spectators with his exuberant personality. He has subsequently appeared in many European opera houses including Covent Garden.

THE VOICE

When I first heard Cura sing at the canal side he was in excellent voice which had a resoundingly rich and luxurious tone which gave the audience and me great pleasure. He displayed an exuberant and humorous personality. I now find that the voice is no longer as vigorous, which I regret while retaining my memories. In Celeste Aida, from Aida by Verdi also disappoints except in the higher range which he seems to have maintained - but it is not the same Cura.

MARIO DEL MONACO

BIOGRAPHY

Born 27 July 1915 in Florence, died 16 October 1982, in Mestre/Venice.

Del Monaco graduated from the Rossini Conservatory at Pesaro where he first met and sang with Renata Tebaldi. At his debut at the Puccini Theatre in Milan on 31 December 1940 he sang the role of Pinkerton in Madama Butterfly. His first appearance at Covent Garden in 1946 made all aware of his powerful metallic voice and led to his stay at New York's Metropolitan from 1951 to 1959. His most popular role was Otello which he sang 427 times. Other operas include Aida, Lohengrin, Marta, Carmen, Manon Lescaut and Pagliacci. In 1975 he retired from the stage and died in Mestre in 1982.

THE VOICE

In the aria Ensultata from Verdi's Otello, del Monaco had a steady strong voice, with good impressive tones. Otello being a very difficult opera to sing, he obviously pushed himself to attain his reach, but did not quite make it. His ringing voice and virile appearance earned him the nickname of the "Brass Bull of Milan". Many criticised him for lack of subtlety and rigid vocal interpretations.

MARIO del MONACO

GIUSEPPE DI STEFANO

BIOGRAPHY

Born 24 July 1921, Motta, Sant 'Anastasia (Sicily); died 3 March 2008, Santamaria, Hoi, near Milan.

De Stefano made his operatic debut in 1946 in Reggio Emilia as Des Gneux in Massenet's Manon and repeated this one year later at his La Scala debut. His New York debut was as the Duke in Rigoletto in 1961, and that year sang Cavaradossi in Tosca at Covent Garden. Later he took on heavier roles which caused his voice to deteriorate and end his career in the late 1960s. In 2004 he was brutally beaten in Kenya and suffered brain damage. Three years later he was flown to Milan and slipped into a coma, dying at his home near Milan.

THE VOICE

Di Stefano was very good in the upper register; his lower register was slightly weaker. He had a rich and typically Italian tone in La Boheme. In Questa O Quella from Rigoletto by Verdi, his voice was very strong especially in the lower range, being particularly good, virile and expressive.

GIUSEPPE di STEFANO

PLACIDO DOMINGO

BIOGRAPHY

Born 21 January 1941, in Madrid.

Domingo grew up in Mexico. In 1957 he made his first professional appearance with his mother, a zarzuela singer and
made his opera debut in a baritone role in Manuel Fernandez
Cavallero's zarzuela Gigantes -y-cabegudos. In 1959 he audi-
tioned for the Mexican National Opera as a tenor and was
accepted. On 12 May that year he appeared as Pasquai in
Marina, and as Borsa in Rigoletto. In 1961 he first appeared in
a leading role in Monterrey, Mexico, as Alfredo in La Traviata;
later, in Dallas, he sang Arturo in Lucia di Lammermoor
opposite Joan Sutherland. At the end of 1962 he started a stay
in Tel Aviv as tenor to the Hebrew National Opera where he
sang 280 performances in twelve different roles.

His next move was to the New York City Opera where his
debut was as Pinkerton in Madama Butterfly followed by
Carmen. At the Metropolitan on 28 September 1968 he sang
Cilea's Adriana Lecoudreur with Renata Tebaldi. He subse-
quently .sang at the Vienna State Opera, the Lyric Opera of
Chicago, La Scala and San Francisco in 1969, and Covent
Garden in 1971. In 1971 he sang in Tosca at the Metropolitan
and since then continues in a wide range of operas worldwide.
In addition he has taken part in the Three Tenors concerts in
their various venues.

THE VOICE

Both in operatic arias and in his performances as one of the Three Tenors he has a clear melodic but slightly dark voice. The sound is rich and the quality impeccable. He sings with great passion and is undoubtedly classed as one of the leading tenors of his generation, which explains his well-deserved popularity. In 2009 he started a new career by switching to baritone roles.

JUAN DIEGO FLOREZ

BIOGRAPHY

Born 13 January 1973, Lima, Peru.

Florez entered the National Conservatory of Music in Lima at the age of 17. His classical abilities developed rapidly and in 1993 he received a scholarship to the Curtis Institute in Philadelphia and specialised in Rossini, Bellini and Donizetti. In 1996 he participated in the Rossini festival in Pesaro where he stepped in to take the leading tenor role in Matilde di Shabaran. The same year he made his debut at La Scala as the Chevalier Danois in Gluck's Armide. In 1998, at his debut at Covent Garden he sang the role of Count Potoski in Donizetti's Elisabetta. and had subsequent debuts at the Vienna State Opera and the Metropolitan. On 20 February 2007 he sang at the opening night of Donizetti's The Daughter of the Regiment at La Scala where he received a rapturous ovation and the unprecedented call for an encore. Florez has been recognised by his homeland with several awards and distinctions.

THE VOICE

Florez, who has a fine voice, which is a little thin and not very dramatic. His high C is often very good but unfortunately becomes a little screechy at times. There is still time for his voice to develop further.

NICOLAI GEDDA

BIOGRAPHY

Born 11 July 1925 in Stockholm.

While Gedda was working as a bank teller, a wealthy client overheard him saying that it was his ambition to sing professionally, and paid for him to study with Carl Maitin Ohman, who had been a well known Wagnerian tenor, and who had discovered Jussi Bjoerling. In April 1953 he made his debut at the Royal Swedish Opera, performing as Chapelou in Adolphe Adams's le Postilion de Longiumeau. Thereafter von Karajan took him to study in Italy; he made his debut at La Scala as Don Ottavio in Don Giovanni. The next year he sang at the Paris opera in Weber's Oberon. His Covent Garden debut followed in 1954 as the Duke of Mantua in Rigoletto. In 1957 he made his Metropolitan debut in Gounod's Faust. He then went on to sing 28 roles over the next 26 years; he continued to sing into his late seventies. Gedda was also a widely recorded tenor.

THE VOICE

Singing the aria Je Croix Entendra Encore from the Pearlfishers by Bizet Gedda displays a fine steady voice. It had beauty, with a warm tone, and the ranges were well sung. In the duet in Mirelle by Gounod he provides an elegant rendition with good quality ranges including a strong high C. Gedda has a good voice and deserves to be listed among the top tenors of his era.

NICOLAI GEDDA

BENIAMINO GIGLI

BIOGRAPHY

Born 20 March 1890, Racanati (Italy); died 30 November 1957, Rome.

Gigli's operatic debut on 15 October 1914 was as Enzo in La Gioconda in Rovigo. After he sang in all the major Italian opera houses he finally appeared at the Metropolitan in New York on 26 November 1920. He achieved international prominence after the death of Caruso. He subsequently returned to Italy and appeared at the major European and South American houses, including La Scala, San Carlo, Covent Garden, the Vienna State Opera and the Teatro de Colon in Buenos Aires. He was best known as Edgardo in Donizetti's Lucia de Lammermoor, Rodolfo in La Boheme by Puccini, and the title role in Andrea Chenier by Giordano. He was very close to his confessor, Padre Pio. He had two children by his wife Constanza; later he had a second family with Lucia Vigarani.

THE VOICE

Gigli sang Le Croix Endendra in La Pechuses de Perles by Bizet very well, considering the age of the recording, he obviously sang with great feeling and empathy. It is a pleasure that his voice retained its colour and beauty. In the lovely song Mamma by Bixio, Gigli allows us to appreciate his great talent that spanned his career; his voice remained beautiful and displayed very good ranges in the tones.

BENIAMINO GIGLI

JAN KIEPURA

BIOGRAPHY

Born 16 May 1902, Sosnowiec, Poland; died 15 August 1966, Harrison, New York.

While undertaking law studies in Warsaw in the early 1920s, Kiepura also took singing lessons. His debut in 1924 was in the Polish opera Halka, but his important appearance was on 11 February 1925 in Faust. The following month Kiepura gained popularity singing in Rigoletto and Cavalleria Rusticana. In Vienna in 1926, he was given the role of Cavadarossi in Tosca which proved a great success. In 1929 he sang Cavadarossi at La Scala. With the political problems in Central Europe, he settled in America and in 1937 he toured in The Merry Widow. The next year saw his debut at the Metropolitan as Rodolfo in La Boheme. He continued to be a popular tenor into his sixties, but died of a heart attack at the age of 64.

THE VOICE

Kiepura's voice had a rich warm tone. He sang roles throughout the tenor range but avoided taxing works like Otello. He was also a prolific singing movie star and was famous for the movie "I Love All Women." (1935).

JAN KIEPURA

ALFREDO KRAUS

BIOGRAPHY

Born 24 September 1927, Las Palmas; died 10 September 1999, Madrid.

Of Austrian descent, Kraus often used his matronymic Trujillo. In 1956 he made his debut in Cairo as the duke in Rigoletto, which became one of his signature roles. Two years later in Lisbon, he sang Alfredo in La Traviata with Maria Callas. In 1959 he first appeared in Covent Garden as Edgardo in Lucia de Lammermoor. The following year, for his La Scala debut, he appeared as Alvino in La Somnambula. He had a wide range of roles but became virtually synonymous with lyric tenor roles like Werther, Faust and Don Ottavio in Don Giovanni. His wife died in 1994 and he stopped performing for eight months; he eventually returned to the stage and to teaching but died after a prolonged illness.

THE VOICE

Kraus had a very pleasant voice which possessed both spinto and lyrical tones which makes for very interesting listening. His lower range was particularly good and had a calming quality. His high register was also excellent. He had very steady control in the rendition of his arias, with precise diction. It has always been a pleasure to listen to him.

Alfredo Kraus as the Duke in Rigoletto
at his Metropolitan Opera debut

MARIO LANZA

BIOGRAPHY

Born 31 January 1921, in Philadelphia; died 7 October 1959, Rome.

Lanza was an American tenor and a Hollywood movie star. At the age of five he frequently listened to records of operas played by his father. He remembered how to operate the gramophone and would listen to it while his father was away. He was able to recall 52 arias at an early age. While still very young he had already decided on an operatic career.

At the age of 17, at the Philadelphia Academy of Music he met Giovanni Martinelli. Later he had the chance to sing for the visiting Serge Koussevitzky, and performed Vesti la Giubba from Leoncavallo's Pagliacci - the maestro embraced him and told him that he had a truly great voice and invited him to Tanglewood, Massachusetts, to study on a full scholarship. When Lanza was 21, Koussevitzky told him "Yours is a voice such as is heard only once in a hundred years."

Towards the end of the war he sang in concerts for the troops and in 1945, from radio shows his voice was heard by a wide audience, which led to movie performances that Louis B. Mayer of MGM put him under contract for several years. Lanza did so well that he delayed the promised music tuition and only appeared in one opera, Madama Butterfly; his large income provided a luxurious lifestyle, but this and stress thwarted his operatic ambitions He suffered severely from critics who were malicious because of his success in movies.

He is best remembered because of his magnificent performance in the movie The Great Caruso. The drastic steps prescribed for his obesity and alcoholic binges harmed him and made him fear that he would lose his voice. He moved to Rome where he died from pulmonary embolism. Armando Cesare's recent biography gives great insights into this largely forgotten tenor who deserves greater recognition; so too does Derek Mannering's "Singing to the Gods." whose opus benefits from his relationship to the Lanza family; I find it the more readable and enjoyable book.

THE VOICE

When I was twelve I became aware of this magnificent voice to which I listened whenever possible. More to the point, his voice was much admired by Joan Sutherland and Richard Bonynge (a voice expert), Jose Carreras, Placido Domingo, Pavarotti and many other contemporaries. In Una Furtiva Lagrima from Donizetti's L'Elisir d'Amore, Lanza astonishes us with a wonderfully exciting, warm and rich spinto voice which expresses great passion. That his voice is darker than some of the other tenors is no disadvantage. His acting was very acceptable and his diction was perfect. His vocal excellence shows that it matters not where one sings, whether in opera, recitals or in the street, for he gave great joy and pleasure to all; in his popular songs he expressed himself with as much quality as in arias.

Mario Lanza

SALVATORE LICITRA

BIOGRAPHY

Born 1968, Bern, Switzerland.

The son of Sicilian parents, he grew up in Milan. He studied in Parma where he made his debut in The Masked Ball in 1998. By March 1999 he had developed an extensive repertoire under Ricardo Muti; he then sang in Tosca and Madama Butterfly in Verona and again in Tosca at La Scala in March 2000. That November he made his American debut, and in December he went to Vienna to sing in Tosca at the State Opera.

On 12 May 2002 he substituted for Pavarotti in Tosca at the Metropolitan. Since then he has added extensively to his repertoire, including Andrea Chenier and Don Carlos.

THE VOICE

Licitra has a splendid luxuriant voice which expresses itself with a well-controlled tone. In Nessun Dorma from Turandot he gives an exciting, indeed exhilarating, rendition in which he easily reaches his ranges to end with a thrilling high C.

GIOVANNI MARTINELLI

BIOGRAPHY

Born 22 October 1885, in Montagnana, Italy; died 2 February 1969, New York.

After service as a clarinetist in a military band, Martinelli studied with Giuseppe Mandolini in Milan. He made his debut at the Teatro dal Verne as Ernani in 1910. His most famous role throughout his life was as Dick Johnson in The Girl of the Golden West, which he sang at La Scala in 1912, as well as for most of his debuts. In 1913 he first appeared at the Metropolitan opera in La Boheme. He remained a mainstay of that company for 32 seasons, singing in 926 performances, most often as Rademes in Aida, Otello and Manrico in Il Trovatore. He sang widely in America and often in Buenos Aires. He was often spoken of as the successor to Caruso. In 1937 he sang Otello at Covent Garden, only retiring from the stage in 1950.

THE VOICE

Martinelli was one of the most popular tenors of his era with a much admired voice. In singing in La Donna e Mobile from Rigoletto he provided a very good rendition, essentially spinto with firm dramatic tones in lower ranges with a slight tinge of the lyrical. His voice was very dark, the upper range suffering from the strain to attain the higher register; at times it was very pleasant but not consistently so.

Martinelli As Manrico In Il Trovatore

BIOGRAPHY

Born 3 June 1904 in New York; died 13 December 1984, New York.

Having already achieved a successful career as a famous synagogue cantor, in 1932 Peerce started as a soloist tenor at Radio City Music Hall and soon developed a nationwide following. He made his operatic debut in May 1938 in Philadelphia as the Duke of Mantua in Rigoletto. Toscanini having heard him singing Wagner on the radio, a recording of the broadcast is among the outstanding musical legacies of the mid twentieth century. He soon became "Toscanini's Tenor". Peerce made his debut with the Metropolitan Opera on 29 November 1941 as Alfredo in La Traviata. In the nineteen fifties he performed regularly as a featured soloist along with such luminaries as Richard Tucker and Robert Merrill, under the baton of Alfredo Antonini. He became the first American to sing with the Bolshoi in Moscow, in 1956, and was a sensation. He remained on the roster of the Metropolitan and 1971 saw him on Broadway as Tevya in Fiddler on the Roof, a new and successful departure. He retired in 1982 and died two years later in New York

THE VOICE

In Don Giovanni Peerce displayed a good Mozartian voice. It was strong and delightfully sung, with good spinto renditions. He held his notes well - they flowed very steadily. Although he was more baritone than tenor he attracted general admiration.

GIANNI RAIMONDI

BIOGRAPHY

Born 17 April 1923, in Bologna; died 19 October 2008, in Pianoro, near Bologna.

Raimondi studied at the music conservatory in his home town, Bologna. He made his stage debut in 1947 in Rigoletto at the Teatro Consorziale in Budrio. The next year he sang as Ernesto in Donizetti's Don Pasquale at the Teatro Comunale di Bologna. Thereafter he toured Italy and in Florence in 1952 revived Rossini's Armida opposite Maria Callas. He made guest appearances in Nice, Marseille, Monte Carlo, Paris and London. At his La Scala debut in 1955 he sang as Alfredo in La Traviata, again opposite Callas. In 1957 he sang as Percy in Donizetti's Anna Bolena, once more with Callas. Later at La Scala he participated in two Rossini revivals, Mose in Egitto (1958) and Semiramide, opposite Joan Sutherland (1962).

In 1957 he made his debut at the Vienna State Opera where he continued to perform during the next twenty years; he sang in Tosca, Madama Butterfly and The Masked Ball. In 1963 he sang Rodolfo to Mirella Freni's Mimi (La Boheme): the conductor was von Karajan. His American debut was at the San Francisco Opera, also in 1957. He also appeared at the Teatro Colon in 1959. He made his Metropolitan debut in 1965 in La Boheme. In retirement he lived in Riccione with his soprano wife and died in Pianoro aged 85.

THE VOICE

Raimondi was a classical lyric tenor. His singing as Rodolfo in La Boheme distinguished himself with a very strong and colourful voice and a good high C in the aria "Your Tiny Hand is Frozen". At times the high C became a little screechy. In the love duet his voice had become a little thin and seemed to have lost some of its lustre. Later, in the crowd scene, and then at the restaurant, he rekindled his voice with some rich tones. These comments apply to early as well as later recordings. On the whole his voice was not altogether as consistent as previously displayed in the first scene. I have heard many better Rodolfos.

TITO SCHIPA

BIOGRAPHY

Born 27 December 1888 in Lucca, Italy; died 16 December 1965 in New York.

Schipa studied in Milan and made his debut in Vercelli in 1910. He then appeared throughout Italy as well as in Buenos Aires where in 1917 he created the role of Ruggiero in Puccini's La Rondine. In 1919 he moved to America, joining the Chicago Opera company and subsequently the Metropolitan Opera, but continuing to perform regularly in Italy. Schipa's repertoire included Massenet's Werther, Donizetti's L'Elisir d' amore and Cilea's L'Arlesiana. In 1932 he made a famous recording of Donizetti's Don Pasquale. Schipa retired from the stage in 1958 to teach in Budapest and subsequently in New York, where he died.

THE VOICE

Schipa has a few patches of attractive singing, with a strong voice, but was not in the class of the great tenors. Nevertheless, over his long career, he gave pleasure to many.

JOSEF SCHMIDT

BIOGRAPHY

Born 4 March 1904, in Davidine, Austro-Hungary; died 16 November 1942, in a Swiss refugee camp near Zurich.

The child of musical parents, he trained to be a cantor at the Czernowitz synagogue (then in Austro-Hungary). At the age of 20 he gave his first recital which included arias by Verdi, Puccini, Rossini and Bizet. His training continued in Berlin to which he returned in 1929 for a radio broadcast as Vasco da Gama in Meyerbeer's L'Africaine. In 1937, after leaving Germany, he toured America together with other famous singers including Grace Moore. After the war broke out he was trapped in France by the German invasion but escaped to Switzerland where he was interned, and died of a heart attack at the age of 38.

THE VOICE

Schmidt was a very pleasant surprise as he was one of my mother's favourite singers. He had a lyric tenor voice and could sail up to a high D. His voice was also perfectly suited for songs by Schubert and Lehar. Though his original training was not in opera he had a very beautiful voice and singing in Reconditte Amore from Tosca gave me great joy as I thought of my mother. His operatic ranges were very good, especially his high C, as one could hear despite the fact that the recording was very old.

LEO SLEZAK

BIOGRAPHY

Born 18 August 1873 in Mahrisch-Schonberg (Austro-Hungary); died 1 June 1946, Rottach-Egern (Bavaria)

Slezak undertook a variety of physical jobs and did military service before taking singing lessons with Adolf Robinson. He made his debut in Brunn in 1896 and sang leading roles in Bohemia and Germany, appearing in Berlin in 1898. In 1901 he became a regular member of the Vienna State Opera. His international career started at Covent Garden where he sang in Siegfried and Lohengrin in 1900. He then undertook further vocal studies in Paris with the famous 19lh century tenor Jean de Reszke. In 1909 he obtained a three year contract with the Metropolitan Opera under Arturo Toscanini where he became the most famous Otello of his generation. He had a repertoire of 66 roles such as William Tell by Rossini, Otello and Rademes. During a European performance of Lohengrin a stage hand sent the swan out too early for Slezak to step aboard, and he quipped "When does the next swan leave?"

THE VOICE

Slezak possessed a large and attractive lyric-dramatic voice with a distinctive tonal quality. His voice was pure and rich with a good baritone range. In the Prize Song from Wagner's Meistersingers he provided a warm and well-controlled rendition with a secure high C; in all a very pleasant voice. Unfortunately in his later years his top register developed a strained quality at full volume. It is however noteworthy that his great qualities can be heard in recordings made in the first decades of the twentieth century.

Leo Slezak, ca. 1927

RICHARD TAUBER

BIOGRAPHY

Born 16 May 1891, in Linz (Austria); died 8 January 1948, in London.

After various minor roles locally and in Dresden in 1922 Tauber signed a contract with the Vienna State Opera and also appeared with the Berlin State Opera. He sang the tenor role in Don Giovanni, The Bartered Bride and Tosca as well as other major works. These included operas by Erich Wolfgang Korngold (Die Tote Stadt) and other modern composers such as Wilhelm Kienzl's Der Evangelimann. In 1924 he sang Armand in Franz Lehar's Frasquita which was a great success and which led to his flourishing career in operetta, that brought him enormous popularity. In 1931 Tauber made his London debut in operetta; among his popular successes were "You are my heart's delight" from the Land of Smiles, and the Merry Widow Waltz, both by Franz Lehar.

Because of his Jewish ancestry he was unable to return to Germany and Austria. He died in London of cancer of the lung.

THE VOICE

Tauber had a flexible lyrical tenor voice and he sang with a warm legato. He also had a unique tone and fortunately his recordings reflect it faithfully. His voice is strong, rich and melodic, and characteristic of a personal nature that differentiates him from other tenors.

RICHARD TAUBER

RICHARD TUCKER

BIOGRAPHY

Born 28 August 1913 in New York; died 8 January 1975, in Kalamazoo, Michigan, USA.

Tucker's aptitude was nurtured by Samuel Weisser at the Tifereth Israel synagogue as a cantor. In June 1943 he became cantor at the Brooklyn Jewish Centre. Sol Hurok had introduced him to the Metropolitan Opera on 29 November 1941. In 1945 he made one of the most successful debuts as Enzo in La Gioconda. Two years later he outperformed Maria Callas in the same opera. Another two years later Toscanini engaged Tucker in the role of Rademes in Aida. However, his voice thereafter started to decline. Ironically Robert Merrill was touring with him when on 8 January 1975 Tucker died of a heart attack.

THE VOICE

Tucker had a most amazing cantorial voice, of tremendous quality, better than that of many other operatic tenors. Hurok had been intensely impressed at the richness of his tone. He exemplified the best of the cantorial tradition while able to sing a wide range of operatic arias. His voice was well suited to the roles of Rodolfo in La Boheme, Pinkerton in Madama Butterfly and Rademes in Aida while also having the cantorial quality of Moyshe Oysher.

RICHARD TUCKER

JON VICKERS

BIOGRAPHY

Born 29 October 1926, in Prince Albert, Saskatchewan, Canada.

In 1950 Vickers was awarded a scholarship to study opera at the Toronto Royal Conservatory of Music. Seven years later he joined the Royal Opera House, Covent Garden, and made his debut as Riccardo in Verdi's Masked Ball and later sang in the Trojans, Rademes in Aida, and Don Carlos. In 1960 he joined the Metropolitan Opera where his debut role was Canio in Pagliacci. He appeared at the Metropolitan for 20 seasons giving 225 performances in 16 roles notably Don Jose Herman in Tchaikovsky's Queen of Spades. He also sang in Bayreuth, at La Scala, Chicago, San Francisco and Salzburg. His basic musicianship was never in doubt; portrayal of tormented figures including Peter Grimes, Otello, and Sampson formed the basis of his artistic heritage.

THE VOICE

Undoubtedly his best feature is the strength of his voice, but it does not give one the thrill that sets apart the great tenors. Furthermore there are strong elements of a baritone background to his tenor notes. On balance he does not fall into the category of the top tenors.

ROLANDO VILLAZON

BIOGRAPHY

Born 22 February 1972 in Mexico City.

At the age of eleven Villazon studied music at the Espacios Academy in Mexico City. In 1990 he met Arturo Niieto who introduced him into the world of opera and became his voice teacher. Two years later he joined the National Conservatory of Music to study under Enrique Jaso. In 1998 he joined the Pittsburg Opera's young artists programme and later studied at the San Francisco Opera where he sang Alfredo in La Traviata. He made his European debut as Des Grieux in Manon, and Rodolfo in La Boheme, in Lyon, France in December 1999. He has subsequently sung a wide variety of roles in many countries.

THE VOICE

Villazon has a very rich, melodic and beautiful voice which he uses in a rather dark and steady tone in an aria in La Gioconda by Ponchielli. In other arias he extends his range to greater strength. His voice extends itself with ease and has a strong musical vocality which makes for a thrilling rendition. He has a very good high C. This is the voice which may take him far in his generation of tenors.

Recently I heard and watched a performance of La Boheme in which he sang Rodolfo. I was rather shocked and puzzled at how his voice had deteriorated as I had originally rated him one of the top tenors of his generation. Rumour has it that he will be returning to the opera house after taking some time off, when one hopes he will be back on form.

FRITZ WUNDERLICH

BIOGRAPHY

Born 16 September 1930 in Kusel (Germany); died 17 September 1966 in Heidelberg.

Wunderlich worked in a bakery, but at the insistence of neighbours he obtained a scholarship at the Freiburg College of Music where he was discovered to be a brilliant young tenor with the full range of lyrical repertoire. He naturally sang in German, including Rigoletto, Don Carlos and The Magic Flute. His promising career was cut short by a fall from which he died at the age of 36. The expectations of his career were thus cruelly thwarted.

THE VOICE

In Mozart's Magic Flute Wunderlich's voice is very lyrical and one detects a lieder tone and wonder whether it would have remained as it was in his operatic singing. His voice was very solid and steady, but also sweet and gentle in other parts of the aria.

FRITZ WUNDERLICH

LUCIANO PAVAROTTI

BIOGRAPHY

Born 12 October 1935, Modena, Italy; died 6 September 2007 in Modena.

After experience as the son of a baker who also sang, Pavarotti abandoned his dream of becoming a footballer. He directly began his career as a tenor and together with his father he entered a competition in Wales, which he won. Early in his career he made his debut as Rodolfo in La Boheme at the Vienna State Opera. In 1965 in America he sang in Donizetti's Lucia de Lammermoor opposite Joan Sutherland. That April Pavarotti made his La Scala debut in Zefferelli's production of La Boheme with Mirella Freni, conducted by Herbert von Karajan. Thereafter he sang in opera houses in Europe and in October 1965, on a visit to Australia, his talent was recognised by Joan Sutherland and her husband Richard Bonynge who helped his development. This led to his being appreciated as a leading tenor by the following year. In 1968 his debut at the Metropolitan opera won him enthusiastic acclaim. In December 1969 his performance in Rome in I Lombardi was another triumph. On 17 February 1972 he sang in The Daughter of the Regiment and produced an effortless high C, to a tremendous ovation. In 1985 he gave his first open air performance in London's Hyde Park, where he dedicated an aria to Princess Diana. Together with Placido Domingo and Jose Carreras, at the 1990 World Football Cup final in Rome they sang as The Three Tenors; his rendition of Nessun Dorma from Turandot entranced the audience, and indeed the world, with his extraordinary high C. This became a feature of future World Cup finals. Apart from this, Pavarotti gave numerous open air performances. Unfortunately the latter part of his career was marred by several cancellations, and in the last few years these were due to ill-health. In 2006 he developed cancer of the pancreas from which he died.

THE VOICE

Pavarotti was at his best in bel canto operas where the brilliance and beauty of his tone, especially in the upper register brought him worldwide fame. The only thing that was lacking was deep passion. His voice and cheerful smile will always be remembered as well as his ever-present white handkerchief. He had a very large voice and always provided his audience with an enthralling experience. His voice had great steadfast control due to skilful breathing. The voice also appealed to the masses and to young people who through him discovered a kind of music that was new to them.

LUCIANO PAVAROTTI

FINAL THOUGHTS

On reflection, having reviewed the tenors of the twentieth century, and having concluded that Mario Lanza was the leading tenor of the first half of the era and Luciano Pavarotti of the second half: but which one is the best overall? Readers and critics will form their own opinions. Having frequently compared the two voices, the author now has no doubt that Lanza is the premier tenor of the twentieth century - he has the more beautiful voice.

Mario Lanza as Lt. Pinkerton in opera Madama Butterfly